conscious divorce

finding freedom through forgiveness

by eileen dunn

Robert D. Reed Publishers • San Francisco, California

Robert D. Reed Publishers
750 La Playa Street, Suite 647
San Francisco, CA 94121
Phone: 650/994-6570 • Fax: 650/994-6579
E-mail: 4bobreed@msn.com
Web site: www.rdrpublishers.com

Designed and typeset by Katherine Hyde
Cover designed by Julia A. Gaskill at Graphics Plus

ISBN 1-885003-62-5

Library of Congress Control Number 00-102827

Produced and Printed in the United States of America

for Julie Mackey

your friendship has blessed my world
beyond measure . . .

for Kraig

just because . . .

contents

This book is written to share the pains and agony of divorce. It is a story of getting through our pain and dealing with our emotions as our marriage disintegrates before our very eyes. We grew up believing in a dream that no longer worked for us. The dream included finding that "one and only" and living happily ever after until "death do us part." We found this not to be the case for us, those of us who walk this journey of divorce.

Many of us have children from these unions. Children that we love and would never knowingly hurt. Yet, somehow this process can become so intense that we forget the long-lasting effect on our children. May these words remind us of their world. We must be as conscious of their inner world as humanly possible. It is our responsibility to help them heal from the pain of their family separation.

This is also a book of love, of renewal. When you are ready, different ways of relating with your former partner can be experienced. This can be done in your own time, at your own speed.

May these words bring comfort.

May you find healing as you walk this frustrating and lonely road.

Warmly,

eileen

the morning
after your marriage,

it's he, she and
the marriage archetype
sitting at the breakfast table ...

it makes for a full house.

the painful decision,
the unavoidable split

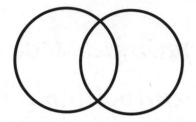

conscious divorce

When a marriage is causing the death of your spirit, a divorce may be the only solution. This decision may be necessary for the spirit of both people to survive. When our spirit is filled with love and joy, we are given the opportunity to express all we can be as human beings on our earth. When we find ourselves in situations that cause the death of our spirit,

we must move on.

We must.

Sometimes, divorce is the path.

I knew.

I knew with all of my heart
and all of my soul,

this marriage was over.
this marriage had died a long time ago.

I had denied this knowledge for quite awhile.

I had pretended I didn't hear
the insistent whisperings in my heart.
I had tried to ignore them,
I had tried to block them out of my mind,

I had worked, harder.
I had exercised, longer.
I had held my baby, closer.

I had tried to make believe
that all was okay,
that all was fine,
and everything was normal.

but, in my heart of hearts,

I knew.

I knew this marriage was over.
that it had died a long time ago.

conscious divorce

we do not
spend quality time,
together.

we do not
make decisions,
together.

we do not even sleep
together.

we live together,
but we do not
discover Life
together.

you do your thing, and I do mine.

we go our separate ways.

together.

we never spoke, my husband and I.

he was not interested
in my thoughts and feelings about life.

HE JUST WANTED DINNER.

he never even noticed that we didn't speak.

I guess he never cared.

but I did.

I needed to connect with him.
I needed to know his heart.
I needed him to know mine.

yet, we never spoke, my husband and I.

I asked him to take a walk with me,
he wouldn't go outside.

I asked him to go away with me,
he wouldn't take a trip.

I asked him to hold me,
he wouldn't come to bed.

conscious divorce

my spirit was dying,
and my loneliness permeated every
aspect of my life.

after awhile,
I no longer cared. I no longer tried.
I had begun to shut down.

I didn't want to take a walk with him.
I didn't want to go away with him.
I didn't ask him to hold me.

I just wanted to be by myself. all by myself.

the painful decision . . .

we tried counseling.
oh my god!!
how many counselors?
was it four or six?

I lost count.
if I trusted one, he didn't.
if he agreed with one, I didn't.
it seemed to be an endless cycle.

it was just a microcosm of our marriage.
we hadn't seen eye-to-eye in such a long time,
how were we to agree on such a critical issue
as who was the best counselor for us?

yet we didn't give up.

as our search continued,
we found ourselves in various offices.

it was a horrible, horrible time.
a time filled with anger and blame,
rage and sorrow.

we both suffered a deep sense of loss
as we watched the death of so many of our dreams.

we *had* to let this marriage go,
we found our paths were too separate.

he had gone his way,
and I had gone mine,
and the two did not intersect.

the paths weren't even on the same map.

the painful decision . . .

he put me in a box. I think a better description would be
A CAGE.

there were certain parameters and certain requirements that formed the boundaries of this ethereal box-cage.

somewhere he had gotten the mind-boggling idea it was his right to tell me exactly how to think about life, who my friends could be, and what beliefs I needed to live by.

it took me awhile to feel the damaging effects of my box-cage. it had been placed so subtly, I had hardly noticed its construction. I had hardly noticed its confinement. I had not understood the strength of its oppression.

eventually, I made an earth-shattering discovery.

I was claustrophobic.

I was suffocating,

I couldn't take a breath.

I needed freedom of thought.
I needed freedom of movement.

I needed **OUT.**

my soul cried,

and I began to listen.

---

you went back to cigarettes
for a year
and I never even noticed.

doesn't that speak volumes?

---

we did not communicate with each other.
we did not listen to each other.
we did not give freedom to each other
to grow and evolve.

somehow, our marriage had become
"the picture"—

"the picture" being the material world we had created,
a world made up of our business and our child.

if you could hold it in your hand
it was part of this picture I speak of.
but, along the journey of picture making,
we had somehow lost touch.

we did not speak of feelings,
we did not share life dreams.
we did not spend quality time together.
we forgot how to laugh with one another.
we forgot how to dance together.

we just existed.

the strength of the "we" became weaker

as I ever so slowly lost touch with my self,

with all of my dreams,
with all of my passions,
and with my heart's true desire.

over the years, I had quit asking myself,
"what do I want?" and I started asking myself,
"what can I do so you won't get so angry?"
and I found there was less and less
I could do or desired to do.

I was getting very tired.

my energy seemed to be dissipating
as our connection was weakening.

*we were becoming strangers
to each other,
even as we lived in the same house.*

we may have shared a beautiful house

but we had quit sharing Life.

the death of our relationship
happened so slowly
that neither of us can pinpoint
the moment of no return.

one day,
we woke up and it was over.

. . . and I grieve.

I always thought it would work out.
there was never any doubt in my mind.

I loved him deeply, he loved me.
my heart knew this to be true.
we wanted to be
together, forever.
why not get married?

I see now
I didn't fully comprehend
the magnitude
of this marriage decision.

I was now bound to live my life
filtered through another.
this was not the problem.

the problem was the one I had chosen.

opposites may attract,
but I found it impossible
for us to grow together.

eventually we realized we had nothing in common,
our internal worlds were universes apart.

we didn't even speak the same language,
and I was lonelier than I ever thought possible.

is it better
to divorce and find peace
or
stay married and be miserable?

I was dying.
I was losing interest in life.
my heart was broken
and my soul, lost.

I was dying,
and I could no longer
participate in the energy dynamics
that we had created.

we had created patterns
of withdrawal,
separation,
isolation.

and for some reason,
there was an awful lot of
yelling.

I was confused,
for I loved him.
I had always loved him,
and I knew I would love him
until the day
I die.

Yet,

I knew we were not good for each other.
I knew we were suffocating each other.
I knew we were causing each other immeasurable pain.

we drained each other of precious life energy.
we were in such destructive patterns
that someone was going to get very sick.

there was no mistaking this.
the signs were all there.

for all to see,
for all the world to see.

―――⋈―――

"till death do us part."

but what do you do if the death is
taking place right before your eyes?

do you just sit around and wait
until the body actually drops?

―――⋈―――

conscious divorce

to continue to experience this Life,
LIFE in the highest sense,
with the highest quality of beauty and joy,

we had to admit, to ourselves and each other,

that we were miserable together.

we had started to believe
Life was just a boring, repetitive experience.

but the real problem was us.

we were miserable together.

we were losing our wonderment for Life.
we were losing our excitement
and our sense of adventure.

we were slowly cutting ourselves off
from the energy of Life
and the energy of each other.

we were miserable.

our relationship had reached a point
of destruction to the spirit of each other.

we had no other choice,
we had to separate.

we just had to give each other freedom.

we had to walk away
from our present world
and our future together.

this was inevitable.

Life is much too precious.

"I WANT A DIVORCE."

WORDSWO

RDSWORDS

the anger ran so deep,

WORDSWO

words spoken,
words shouted,
words flung at each other like daggers.
words, that broke hearts
and ripped open our souls.

RDSWORDS

how do relationships disintegrate so?

WORDSWO

how can you love someone,
create a life together,
live in a home,
have a child,

RDSWORDS

*and then be a willing participant in the
crushing of their souls?*

WORDSWO

RDSWORDS

conscious divorce

you took my past
and I am so angry.

I was so naïve to believe in this.
I saw only what I wanted to see,
not what was really happening.

and now you smashed my future.
there were too many dreams
wrapped up here.

too many hopes are now shattered.

I hate this.

my world makes no sense to me.
I am caught in a very bad nightmare.
Col. Mustard did it with a knife in the den.
I never even went into the den,
much less grabbed a knife.

I despise you.

I do not want to see you
or talk with you.

all I want
is for you to go away,
just be

. . . . *GONE.*

if you lost a hundred-dollar bill
while walking in the park . . .

you would be **spitting mad!**

imagine the intensity of anger
we feel when we lose . . .

our marriage,

which is a million times more precious
than any hundred-dollar bill.

you called me 27 times today.

why on earth would you do that?

leave me alone.

leave me alone.

leave me alone.

do not call me 27 times in a day, again.

do not do it.

this needs to stop.

NOW!

friends.

my friends.

your friends.

friends of
the family.

there is a compelling urgency to divide
all friendships into camps.

there is "her camp," and "his camp."

each friend will be assigned to a camp
based on whose friend they were
prior to the marriage.

if the friendship was cultivated
after the marriage,
this makes it a bit more tricky.
it will then depend
on the active enlistment of him or her.

all friends involved
must understand and fully appreciate
they have now entered a **war zone.**
any contact with the other spouse is
completely forbidden.
the occupants in the other camp
are enemies.

there will be no fraternizing between camps.

once a camp is assigned,
you may not switch camps.

although unspoken, *these rules are written in stone.*

conscious divorce

how can you possibly
know my every move?

do you have spies everywhere?

you seem to know
what I'm going to do,
where I'm going to go,
and with whom I'll be going
before I even know.

who are the spies?
where do the betrayers hide?

I remember when you told me
you wanted me

DEAD.

I didn't know what to say,

but I didn't believe it then,

and I don't believe it now.

be careful of the words
you speak,

they may come back
to haunt you.

I knew only sadness.

ALL had shattered,
my past seemed meaningless,
my future so doubtful.
my dreams were broken.
some days, I was not even sure
I could live without you.

I was overwhelmed with grief.

I was afraid and lonely.

I hated the thought of divorce,

yet,

I hated the thought of staying together.

my heart was shattered and my head was pounding.
it seemed as if I was caught in a black hole,
a swirling, whirling massive space of nothingness.

and I knew there was no easy answer,
no quick solution.

aspirin didn't dull the pain at all.

Sometimes,

I miss seeing your brown hiking boots
in the hallway.

before,
when I came home
from a long day at work
and saw your brown hiking boots,
I felt safe. I felt protected.

now,

your hiking boots don't live here anymore.

---

we know in our own
particular situation

we have no other choice,

we must move on.

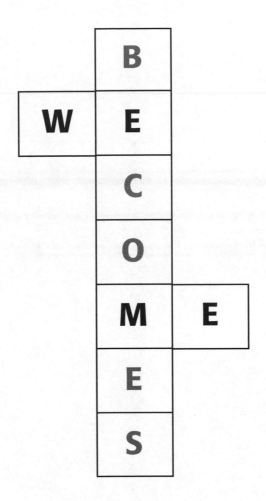

the legal headaches

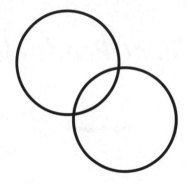

conscious divorce

The divorce process has begun. It now becomes a swirling whirlpool of legal documents and battles fought through lawyers and played out in the court system. The process is time-consuming, expensive, and draining.

Yet we found this process to be a necessary path.

Be quite gentle with yourself.
Remember to take it one day at a time.

"I Do."

two small words.

I hate the nauseating pain
we have to live through
because we spoke
those two small words.

this morning,
I brought $2500
to the lawyer as a retainer.

I DID IT!

the process
begins.

I remember
the day I was served the divorce papers
while I was at work.

I felt as if an atom bomb
was detonated in my body.

it was an explosion of such magnitude
that every cell in my body
was reeling from the effects.

how could I have such a reaction?
why would I have such an intense reaction?

I knew we were getting divorced.
I wanted this.
I knew we had no choice.

we had struggled with this decision
for a long, long time.

we had tried everything we could do
to save this marriage.

but in the end,
we found there wasn't anything
else we could do.

I was ready for the divorce.
or so I thought,

until I lived through the moment
when I was served the papers at work.

this moment is forever frozen in my memory.

the papers contained the most difficult words
I had ever read.

I could not breathe.
I could not talk.
I could only sob.

I had to get outside,
but where could I go?

there was no escaping the anguish of
those words written on that piece of paper,
delivered by a stranger
on a rainy day in September.

there was no escaping this reality of divorce.
I had nowhere
to go.

the legal headaches

one of us is a plaintiff
and one of us is a respondent.
whatever happened to being

you and me?

conscious divorce

you bring out the worst in me.
you bring out the darkest aspects
of my inner being.

I feel rage,
deep, cold rage.
the "I-never-want-to-see-you-again" rage.
the "I-hate-you" rage.
I've been angry and out of control.

I feel isolated,
I feel cut off from the love of the Universe,
cut off from friends and laughter.
I've been lost and alone.

I feel separated
from God and the angels,
from everything I hold dear.
I am like a leaf blowing in the wind.

should I act upon my "worst"
and cause great destruction and pain to you?

or should I thank you for showing me
the parts of my being that need healing?

yes, you bring out the worst in me!

the people we were in this marriage
and the people we are in this divorce
seem to be unrelated.
there seems to be a total lack of congruency.

it's not that the marriage was perfect,
but surely the threads of the marriage
had some beautiful weavings.

I hold many memories
filled with love and respect,
good times and creative impulses.

what has happened?
I now find myself facing an opponent
engaging in horrible, horrible battles.

the characters in this plot seem so foreign to me . . .

even I am foreign.
how have I arrived in this war?

when was I drafted?

conscious divorce

some day,
I will be separate from you.
with my own responses,
my own way of seeing the world,
my own thoughts.

without filtering them through yours.

the knowledge of that day
makes this whole stinking mess
worth the time,
trouble,
cost,
and destruction.

because someday,

I will be free.

did you tell all that crap to the lawyer?
I've never heard such ridiculous nonsense in my life.

I really want to know,
did you actually walk into his office,
sit down on his leather chair,
and spew this stuff?
or did your lawyer
use some form of "lawyer's poetic liberty"
and embellish on some form of the truth
that you gave?
I need to know.
I need to know this
because one of you is

WRONG!

and instead of having a
reasonable conversation that would take,
ohhh, about 15 minutes
to resolve this matter,

it now has become a petition,
a counter petition,
a court date,
a legal guardian,
and a hell of a lawyer bill.

all because the *truth* has not been told.

is it possible to sit
with both lawyers and each one of us,
and have a mature and intelligent conversation?

or do we have to play the court script out?

I have a feeling,
I know the ending
to that particular story.

neither of us wins.
we both lose.

and

the sum of our loss

is greater than any one part.

the battle seems to go on and on.
days, weeks, months, years.

do you realize the absurdity of this?
and at the same time,
the absolute necessity of this?

I have to stand up for what I believe in.
I have to have the freedom to be who I am.
our lives on this planet are over
far too quickly,
so I have to fight for this.

but, god, I hate it.
I hate this.

I hate this whole lawyer thing.

does she even care one iota about me,
or am I just another case to her?

it seems she must get bored
listening to people complain
about their broken marriages.

I despise
that our court system tells me
I need to hire a lawyer to be my voice.

why is *my* voice not enough?

why is my voice not good enough?

I am only trying to get to the truth of the situation.

the whole truth,
and nothing but the truth.

so help me god.

lawyers.
court times.
petitions.

the rest of your life
is put on hold
as you walk this journey
of anger, pain,
separation and loss.

and it's sickening
that lawyers benefit
as they keep the argument going.

the word "truth" was never spoken.
the word "fair" was never uttered.
the word "compromise" was not in their world.

in this cold world
of lawyers,
court times,
and petitions.

these dishes are mine.
I will fight you for them.
I will steal them from you
in the dark of the night.

I WANT MY DISHES.

you cannot have them.
don't even think about it.
my lawyer says the dishes are
mine.
mine, not yours,
MINE.

I pay $600 for four hours
of my lawyer's time
to make absolutely sure
I get the dishes.

have I completely lost my mind?

in the quiet of the night,
I admit to myself,
I don't really care about the dishes.

I don't really give a damn about the dishes,
it's just that they do symbolize something to me,
something I am too afraid to put into words.

I catch a fleeting vague idea,
something about food, sharing meals, family.
and that's as clear about this symbolizing
as I care to get at the moment.

I will not try to find the exact meaning
because how can I know?

I am stuck in blinding anger
and this taints every decision,
every demand I force.

it's so much easier to demand the dishes.
I have control over this.
since I cannot demand this marriage work out,

for now, I'll settle for the dishes.

I can hold the dishes,
I cannot hold this marriage.

I want the dishes.
I want my dishes.
I want **you NOT** to have the dishes.

and so I fight for the damn dishes.

and lo and behold, when all is said and done,
I am awarded the dishes.

and we both go home.
home,
to our separate homes.

so did I go home
and enjoy those hard-earned dishes?

did I eat fine meals surrounded by family?

heck no,
you see, I went home,
to my separate home,
and I smashed every dish.
every one of them.

even the butter dish.

CRASH,
CRASH,
BANG!!!

the lawyers.

thousands and thousands of dollars.
WASTED.

but don't worry,
my lawyer took care of herself.
she bought a new Lexus,
a blue SRV
with four-wheel drive.
cash.

I signed on the dotted line

and this marriage was over.
it only took a moment,
not even a minute.
it was just a quick scribble,

a hastily written signature and
poof,
everything was settled.
all of the paperwork was finished,
and this marriage was officially over.

wait, I have one more question,
where is the paper
I need to sign on the dotted line
to poof away the damage?
to poof away the scars?

my pen is ready,
but my lawyer has already left the room.
where do I go to get this paper?

I forgot to ask.

the papers have been signed.

all this chaos has been channeled
into one final legal paper.
all that is required now is two signatures,
just two signatures.

there, *I've signed the paper.*

now, what I need to know,
is it possible
to heal from this traumatic experience?

both of us have been to hell and back
and often, we've taken our children
and a few of our friends for the ride.

*was this a very bad nightmare,
or did it really happen?*

my world is upside down
and my sense of reality is a bit askew.

I am emotionally drained,
financially poorer,
and sad.

I am very sad.

even with all of this sorrow,
I **know** this was necessary,
but, oh my god!
I am so empty.

I sit and wonder at this turn of events.

I feel a deep sense of rightness about this.

I have faith all will work out.

I have peace.

yes, I admit it seems
to be fleeting peace,
but it is peace nevertheless.

I remember
the day I said,

"I do."

but, in the end,
I didn't.

I just couldn't.

I have left this marriage
broken financially.

I have left this marriage
materially bankrupt.

but I have my freedom.

I have my courage.

I have my daughter.

I will do just fine.

remembering the children

conscious divorce

Going through a divorce is one of the most difficult of life's journeys. During this process, we begin to understand the magnitude of the effect this decision will have on all the members of our family. After the divorce is decreed, everybody's life will be completely different. Nothing will look the same or feel the same. Something extremely precious has been lost.

This agonizing loss is felt by all, but especially our children, our beloved children. The following words are written to remind us of their fragility and vulnerability as we face this deep loss together on a day-to-day basis. We begin the healing process. We begin to pick up the shattered pieces and move onward.

We listen.

We love.

We heal.

the childhood
of the children
rests in our hands.

let us remember their innocence.

she is not "mine . . ."
she is not "yours . . ."

there is no **ownership** here.
nobody owns anybody.

I am her mother forever.
you are her father forever.
she is her own person.

she loves me dearly.
she loves you dearly.

let's just keep this straight.

this is her world.
take off your shoes,
and enter gently.

we have a child,
a blessed, blessed being,
an angel from the heavens.

she blesses
my world with goodness
and endless joy.

she brings
love and sweetness
to my life.

she is my everything.

she is my greatest teacher.
she also teaches another.

he is the father of our child.
he is her father.
he is her father.
he is her father.

this soon becomes my daily mantra,
he is her father.

sometimes,
I have to tell myself this
two thousand times a day.

he is her father.

he is her father and he has
just as much of a right
to raise her
as I do.
he has just as much of a right
to influence her world
and be with her
as I do.

my ego is repulsed by this idea,
by the very thought.

yet, at the same time,
my heart gently
assures me,
this is Truth.

he is her
FATHER.

you raise our child differently than I do.
in a situation when I say "yes,"
you say "no."
when I say, "sure, go out."
you say, "stay home."
when I say
"that's too expensive, you can't have it."
you buy her two.

we don't do this on purpose.
we don't try to have
two completely opposite points of view.
it's just that we have
different parenting styles.
we hold different values, set different rules,
and have an amazingly different way of
looking at the world.

after much thought and prayer,
I realize I respect you enough
to acknowledge
your love for our child.

I pray to give you the freedom
to raise her "your way"
when she is with you.

conscious divorce

I come to accept that I will
not interfere with your parenting.

I will not interfere.
I will not question.

I will not interfere.
I will not question.

(I had to write this ten thousand times,
but I do believe I've got it now.)

I will not interfere.
I will not question.

to treat you
with fairness and kindness
when you are being so unreasonable
makes me feel like I am going to

EXPLODE.

I feel my blood pressure rising.

180/110.

160/95

140/90

my gut tells me,
just scream at him.
just lash out at him.
react harshly.
make him hurt
as much as I hurt.

but my heart has a different idea.

my dear, dear heart,
my sane, sane friend,
tells me to take a moment,
close my eyes, and
realize the immeasurable pain
and total confusion
this behavior brings to our child.

when I look into her green eyes,
I see her unconditional love for you.
I see her spiritual connection with you.
I feel your importance to her.

Today,
I will see you through her eyes.
I really will.

do not use our child to get back at me.

do not criticize who I am to her.
do not try to "buy" her love.
do not create "sides" for her to "choose."

this plan will only
backfire on you.

you may not see
the consequences
of your actions
for years to come.

you may not understand the effect
this behavior will have on her psyche.

but, the day will come
when you will have to face the consequences
of using our child to get back at me.

because, one day,
she will find the words
to verbalize her suppressed rage,
and express her excruciating pain.

but you will have
already stolen
her childhood,
a childhood you so
carelessly discarded.

she is so loved
that our love for her
could fill the universe
a million trillion billion times.

she is precious and she is kind.
she has a gentle and loving heart.
her presence blesses our worlds.

this I know.

this is her childhood,
her one and only childhood,
a time of learning to trust the world
and the people in her life.

this I know.

she has only one childhood.
let us treat it with love,
respect and dignity.

let us not bring harm to her soul
or destroy her childhood
during this divorce process.

her experience of childhood
will influence every decision she makes
for a very long, long time.

this I know.

she is innocent.

in this raging battle
we have undertaken,
she is innocent.

she did not pick up a sword,
she did not enlist soldiers.
she did not cause destruction or pain.
she did not bring harm to anyone.

she played with her Barbie dolls,
made up beautiful songs,
and built sand castles.

she gave both of us
warm hugs and loving kisses,
and pictures drawn with her crayons.

she is innocent.

this *is* something we both know.
this *is* something we both agree upon.

she is innocent.

---

take her tiny hand in yours
and respect her vulnerability.

---

she's at your house tonight.
for the first night since her birth,
I am away from her.
my house is quiet—
very quiet, too quiet.
I miss the chattering of her voice.
I miss her constant questions.
I miss our game of "alphabet soup."
I am full of nervous anxiety.

the beating of my heart is so fast
I feel as if I've just had two double lattes.

how am I ever going to be able
to do this on a weekly basis?

I briefly wonder if the courts have an answer
to this burning question.
I feel as if I haven't seen her in a year.
there is a physical pain from this separation.

what did she have for dinner?
did she enjoy her bath?
did you wash her hair?
what bedtime story did you read to her?
(we're reading *The Secret Garden*.)

I'm lonely.
I miss her terribly.

I'm sad.

conscious divorce

I decide I'd like a warm bath.
so I fill the tub with very warm water,
bubbles, and lavender oil.

I find some peace in this.

I walk hesitantly to her room
and sit on her unmade bed.

I have to move Softerina
from the pillow.
(I briefly wonder if she can sleep tonight
without her favorite toy-friend.)

I put "Fairy Ring" on the stereo.
the music plays so tenderly.

soon the room is filled
with tranquillity and familiarity.
we play this particular music every night.

I sit in her room.
in the silence of her room
I sit.

I am feeling so many emotions
that I cannot decipher all of them.

I am overwhelmed by the turn of events
that happened in my life.

how did this happen
that I have to be away from my daughter?

this divorce brings such pain to me
that I cannot take a breath.
my gut feels like a horse just kicked me,

and I ache from the loneliness of it all.

what does a mom do when her child is away?

my mind cannot answer this question.
my heart cannot answer this question.

I ask the Universe,

"what does a mom do when her child is away?"
at the moment, I don't hear any answers.

the silence
engulfs me
as I fall into
restless sleep
with my head
on her pillow,
Softerina
in my arms,
and tears
on my face.

I didn't see her standing behind me.
I didn't hear her come into the room.

I was too wrapped up
in the conversation
with the lawyer.

and now
she has heard every word,
every word of the grown-up conversation.

**she should have
never EVER
heard those particular words.**

as I hold her in my arms, she cries.
she can hardly catch her breath.
her deep sobs rip at my heart.

all of our hearts are broken,
and some days, it feels like
our hearts just keep getting

SMASHED

into smaller and smaller pieces.

this day, this conversation,
has proven to be especially difficult,
and I cannot take the words back.

we cannot pretend she didn't hear them.
I just didn't hear her come into the room.

My beloved child,

How can I help you understand that you had nothing to
do with our divorce?

How do I find the words to explain such grown-up
decisions to such a little person? I feel inadequate as
I try to tell you about the upcoming changes that our
family is going through.

Some days the only thing I can do is hug you and hold
you and give you assurance that you are loved, and you
will be safe. I don't know what else to tell you . . .

I love you honey,
mom

P.S. No, baby, I don't hate your father.

choosing to forgive,
learning to be friends

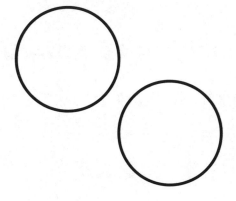

conscious divorce

There are enormous soul lessons that we learn on this planet. Often we do not know the reason why certain events transpire. Our level of trust in the workings of the Universe is an absolute requirement here. No matter the picture, the union with your partner taught you many lessons. No matter how shattering or overwhelming it may seem, you learned something.

Knowing when to walk away from a destructive relationship is one of the greatest lessons we can understand. It takes a great sense of self-love to know when it is time to leave. Sometimes through lack of self-love and self-respect we learn the greatness of these qualities. We realize the absolute necessity of having a loving and supportive relationship.

As time passes on, we begin to see the reasons and gifts of our union. We begin to forgive and find peace.

We move on.

there comes a moment,

when the fighting crosses the line
from necessary expression
to just pure destruction,
for it no longer serves any purpose.

there comes a moment,

when it's time to put away the boxing gloves,
it's time to rest the egos,
time to compromise,
time to accept.

there comes a moment,

when peace begins to fill our heart as
we are filled with compassion and acceptance.

everyone takes a very long,
very overdue, deep breath.

*do not let this particular moment
pass unnoticed.*

conscious divorce

you know my heart,
you know my dreams,
my hopes and my desires.
you know what is important to me.
you are familiar with my spirit,
and now you know my vulnerability.

you know my weaknesses,
you have seen me at my lowest,
you have known me through my darkest hours,
you have helped me pick up the pieces,
and now you know my fragility.

you know my thoughts,
you know my soul.
and now you know my fears.

you can use this information to destroy me
or you can use this information to help me fly.

this particular choice is yours . . .

when I was taking a walk last night,
I had a realization.
this realization almost knocked me over.

I had to sit down on a log.
I had a flash. I was given a great insight.

this is my divorce.
I pray it is the only divorce
I will have to go through
in this lifetime.

therefore,
I need to do this right.
I need to be conscious.
I need to be centered.
I need to use this experience
as a way to "know myself."

it's my one and only divorce
and I am going to do it my way.
I choose to heal through this.

I pray to let go of reacting to your responses.

you see,
you know me so well,
that you know exactly what buttons to push
to get a certain response from me.
and over and over,
I fall into this same stupid game.

I pray to stay centered
and bring healing to this process.

I pray to bring respect
and compassion
for all of us,
for myself, for you, and for our child.

I pray to bring love here,
to our situation that now
is consumed with anger and rage,
hurt and pain.

I pray for courage, strength, and patience.

I must bring these qualities.
here. now.

before it's too late.

the time is now.
I can feel this is the moment.

maybe I slept through the marriage,
but I will not sleep through this divorce.

I want to feel all of my emotions,
the fear, the loneliness,
the freedom, the pain,
the anger, and the relief.

I want to feel it all.
I need to feel it all.

this is not an easy request,
I understand that.

but I want to participate in Life.
I want to be alive,
to be a part of every moment.
to do this, I am convinced

I must fully and completely
feel
my
emotions.
this is essential to my evolution.

I want to feel the entire range of my emotions.

I pray to feel every emotion,
the good, the bad, and the ugly.

I pray to feel alive.
I want to know Life
with every cell of my being.

I accept feeling my pain and sorrow
so that I may also experience true joy
during my lifetime.

you see, I do not want to be numb anymore.

I want to have a conscious divorce.
I want to "know myself" through this process.
I need to bring closure to this chapter in my life.

in order to do this, my heart tells me,
I need to take responsibility
for my actions and my part
in the demise of our marriage.

I need to carefully look at my patterns
and understand how they contributed
to our divorce.

I need to let go of my anger and pain.

these particular requests, directed from my heart,
are among the most difficult lessons
I have been given on this planet.

I find I have great difficulty with this.

my ego wants to blame and find fault with you.

my ego wants to lash out and remember every time
you "wronged" me.

my ego does not want to accept the notion
that I could have done
anything injurious.

I find that none of this is pleasant to ponder
on this Friday afternoon.

conscious divorce

let's heal our relationship.
deeply, thoroughly heal.
let's stop the blaming
and the need to be right.
let's put away our boxing gloves.

let's heal through this
divorce.

come on,
we have no desire
to spend another lifetime
doing this again,

**DO
WE?**

yada da da ya da da
yada da da da da da
he did.
she did.
he did.
I did.
me, too…

life is too short
to play this blame game.

let's just accept
we each played a role
in this dynamic
that caused
deep pain
and horrific communication
and it would benefit each of us
to heal
that piece in us
that caused
this pain
and didn't know how to talk about it.

each of us.

me, no more than you.
you, no more than me.

a reason for being.

sometimes, on this human dimension,
we come to earth
to learn specific lessons.

some of our lessons may teach us
how to respect our self,
how to listen to our heart,
how to follow our passion.
when we find ourselves
in a life situation that is
destroying our self-respect,
denying our heart,
and ignoring our passion,

we have to make the difficult decision
to leave a relationship.

sometimes, we have to go deep, deep
within our hearts and our self
and choose a direction
that will heal us and give us freedom.

we found we had to take this path alone.

a commitment to search the soul,
to travel inward,
is not easy.

it has never been easy.

it takes great courage
to make the necessary changes
in your physical world
that allows
your inner world to embrace life.

*tread lightly
as you listen
deep within your heart,*

in a place called heaven.

this relationship did not fill my needs
nor did it fill your needs.

it left a huge hole in my soul.

it's nobody's fault.
unfortunately, I grew in one direction
and you grew in another,

and our paths never did intersect.

let's just accept this
and let go of the blame game.
this blaming will only keep the wound open,
and the opportunity to heal will be lost.

Life is too short to blame and finger-point.

I have put my accusations away,
and I have accepted my role
in all of this.

I see how some of my patterns
contributed to the destruction
of this marriage.

I've taken off my sunglasses,
and I'm seeing my patterns
more and more clearly.

I take responsibility for them.

I choose to heal them.
I pray to heal them.

our relationship
is a weaving
of a different blanket
than I had originally imagined.

there are broken threads
and a few holes,
but as I look back
on our years of connection,

I find great beauty.

there are many good memories,
many joyous occasions,
many simple times shared.

you have been there to fix my tire.
you have made me coffee hundreds of times.
yes, we have shared a
"history."

we have accomplished
a great deal together,
and this can never be taken away.

our history is ours to carry.

I have received
from our partnership
gifts and jewels about life
that exceed my wildest dreams.

I have truly learned a great deal.

I take this with me as I travel onward.
and for this, I am eternally grateful.

our "blanket" brings me comfort.

I loved you with all of my heart,
as I still do.
yet we couldn't stay married.
I'm sorry.
I am so sorry.

it's not anyone's fault,
we are two very different people
walking this planet.

we are not monsters
trying to destroy each other's life.

we are just different,
as different as night and day.
we have different life goals,
and different life purposes.

ours simply did not mesh together.

I know we made the right decision.
there is a rightness about this.

but I want you to know,
I am devastated at our decision.
I am filled with an incredible sense of loss.

the lump in my throat
makes it impossible to swallow.
the heaviness in my heart
is immeasurable.
we had no choice,

but I am so sad.

I'm sorry.
I am so, so sorry.

may we both heal.

after hours and hours
of meditation, prayer, and
all-around pondering,

I come to know,
know with every cell
of my being,
that in order to heal
I have some choices to make.

I take a very careful look
at my different options.

I spend a lot of time looking
at my different options,

and my choices are made.

conscious divorce

in the quiet of my heart I realize,

I choose to let go of my anger.
I choose to remove any blame
from each of us.
I choose to be fair and kind.
I choose to forgive
myself and you.

I choose to grow and evolve.

I know from the depths of my soul,
I want a peaceful life.

I want this with all of my heart.

and I understand I cannot carry
deep resentment, blame, or guilt
and have a peaceful life
and a healthy body.

I am amazed to know

that by forgiving
you,

I forgive me.

by forgiving you,
my life is greatly blessed.

I make the choice
to heal my broken heart
and my broken life.

it is a difficult
but necessary decision.

I pray
to the angels
for guidance.

I surrender.

indescribable peace fills my being.

I am surrounded by quiet.

all I can hear
is the sound of my own heart.

I feel love for you,
for myself,
and for so many others.

I am remembering how to dance,

a gentle slow dance.

there is nothing wrong with you.
there is nothing wrong with me.

our problem is the energy dynamic
that we create, together.

our differences cannot be resolved.
you see the world your way,
and I see the world my way.

let us accept this and make peace with each other.

it was nice to talk with you last night.
it had been awhile and I had been wondering
how you were doing.

I love talking to you about our daughter.
she sure is growing up fast, isn't she?

I enjoyed sharing a joke with you.
your jokes have always made me laugh.

I want you to know,
I hope for you the very best.
I want you to be happy,
as happy as humanly possible.

I want you to be full of excitement
and wonderment at the world.

I really want this for you.

when we were finished talking,
it also felt very right for me
to hang up the phone,
and be in my own space.

I absolutely know we made the right decision.

as painful as it was,
it was necessary.
so very, very necessary.

in this space of forgiveness,

I am so grateful
we are developing a new friendship.
we are finding a new sense of love
and respect for each other.

our expectations have changed
and I feel the peace we are finding in this.

with distance and separation,
we are recognizing that our connection
continues even as we let go of our marriage.
a new and gentle friendship
is emerging.

I miss you.

maybe we can catch a movie next Tuesday?

sometimes,
a movie is only a movie.

I'll buy the popcorn and Milk Duds.

I have a vision.

I have been seeing this vision for years.

this vision has greatly influenced our relationship.
it has given me the determination
to have a friendship with you
based on respect.

this vision has given me the desire
to go back to the "communications board"
with you on countless occasions.

my vision,
that grabbed me
and wouldn't let me settle
for less than total forgiveness of each other.
(close your eyes and imagine
this powerful and demanding vision—)

we will dance together
at our daughter's wedding.

it will be a fine dance.
it will be a dance of celebration.
it will speak of family connections.
it will be gentle and kind,
it will be from our hearts.

and when we are finished,
we will toast to her happiness,
and she will smile a knowing smile.
and so shall we.

you and I have history together.

we have been together
through so many good times
and so many difficult times.

we have spent a great deal of our time together.
we have been through the birth of our child.
we have been each other's safety,
we have also let each other down.
we have hurt each other,
we have been angry with each other.

together, we have experienced so much of life,
both good times and difficult times.

it's been quite a ride, our friendship,
and even though it's worked out this way,
I just want you to know,
I love you.

I will always **love** *you.*

my beloved soul family,

as we walk this lonely and painful road,

may we all
begin to remember
we are one.
may your journey
know Love.
may your journey
know Peace.
may your journey
reveal your Purpose.

in gentleness,
eileen

Books Available From Robert D. Reed Publishers

Please include payment with orders. Send indicated book/s to:

Name:_____

Address:_____

City:_____ State:_____ Zip:_____

Phone:(_____)_____ E-mail:_____

Titles and Authors	Unit Price
Conscious Divorce: finding freedom through forgiveness by Eileen Dunn	$9.95
Sacred Goodbyes: honoring and healing your pain and loss by Eileen Dunn	9.95
Gotta Minute? How to Look & Feel Great! by Marcia F. Kamph, M.S., D.C.	11.95
Gotta Minute? Practical Tips for Abundant Living: The ABC's of Total Health by Tom Massey, Ph.D., N.D.	9.95
Gotta Minute? Yoga for Health, Relaxation & Well-being by Nirvair Singh Khalsa	9.95
Gotta Minute? Ultimate Guide of One-Minute Workouts for Anyone, Anywhere, Anytime! by Bonnie Nygard, M.Ed. & Bonnie Hopper, M.Ed.	9.95
A Kid's Herb Book For Children Of All Ages by Lesley Tierra, Acupuncturist and Herbalist	19.95
House Calls: How we can all heal the world one visit at a time by Patch Adams, M.D.	11.95
500 Tips For Coping With Chronic Illness by Pamela D. Jacobs, M.A.	11.95

Enclose a copy of this order form with payment for books. Send to the address below. Shipping & handling: $2.50 for first book plus $1.00 for each additional book. California residents add 8.5% sales tax. We offer discounts for large orders.

Please make checks payable to: Robert D. Reed Publishers. Total enclosed: $_____. See our website for more books!

Robert D. Reed Publishers

750 La Playa, Suite 647, San Francisco, CA 94121
Phone: 650-994-6570 • Fax: 650-994-6579
Email: 4bobreed@msn.com • www.rdrpublishers.com